To Sweeten Bitter . Raymond Antrobus

Published by Out-Spoken Press

First edition published 2017

ISBN: 978-0-9931038-7-2

Design & Art Direction
Ben Lee

Printed & Bound by:
Print Resource

Typeset in: Baskerville

Supported by
ARTS COUNCIL
ENGLAND

To Sweeten Bitter

Contents

Foreword

From the very title of this affecting poetry collection, to its final lines, where well-chosen spaces speak loudly what cannot be said, it is clear that Raymond Antrobus knows the value of words that are too precious to squander.

These are poems that are unafraid to be tender, yet are free from sentimentality. These are poems aching with the loss of a father, to dementia even before death, and Raymond Antrobus in these pages moves skilfully between the reclaiming and letting go of memory, transforming intimate hurt into anger and vulnerability and strength and laughter and compassion. Long after I had read the whole collection, resonances of the title poem, "To Sweeten Bitter", with its poignant opening, remained with me:

> *My father had four children*
> *and three sugars in his coffee*
> *and every birthday he bought me*
> *a dictionary, which got thicker*
> *and thicker and because his word*
> *is not dead, I carry it like sugar*

The magic of good poetry has to do with what it is able to say also between the lines, and Raymond Antrobus succeeds in conjuring up a lexicon of emotions evoked by the experiences, observations and history that craft his identity, drawn from a world that may as naturally includes a classroom in Kenya, a boat trip down Jamaica's Black River, a confrontation at Miami airport, as familiar home life in Hackney, east London.

> *Plantation lineage, World War service, how do I serve Jamaican British?*
> *When knowing how to war is Jamaican British.*

Occasional light references to other writers - from Louise Bennett, James Berry to Binyavanga Wainaina and Derek Walcott - give me confidence that here is someone who knows what it takes to follow this literary vocation. Having begun my career as a publisher with poetry, decades ago, I rejoice that Out-Spoken have taken on Raymond Antrobus, a poet so obviously destined for greater things.

Margret Busby OBE *Writer & Publisher*

It is not him walking
up the road in that green,

but you follow his oak face
into the garden where his voice

is still slowly growing spaces
too wide without him.

The air is not his blue coat,
his coat is dust and wood smoke.

Hold   your tremble,
the man walking the road
is not

          your ache.

His Heart

turned against him in a chicken shop
he said *my heart is falling out*

as he slipped into dreams
of his mother in Jamaica

he came through in hospital, longing
for that woman, dead twenty years

his son visits and they spend
half an hour holding hands

there is a needle in his arm
and blood in his colostomy bag

he asks the nurse if he can go to the post office
to buy his daughter a postcard

but forgiveness does not
have an address

Madge is the first girl he kissed in Jamaica –
white floral dress, scent of thyme and summer

she visits his hospital dreams
Madge is not the nurse who dissolves

painkillers in his water
he does not drink with his eyes open

his son turns on the radio,
it is *A Rainy Night In Georgia*

his son, a blur
on a wooden chair.

In The Supermarket

I noticed they sell his toothpaste
and the hair gel he used
so I picked up
everything I used
to see in his house.

The things from aisle 5
surrounded him,
brought him back
but I did not buy
anything in those aisles.

I would be holding
on too hard
to my humming father,
who is wind and mirror
and West Indian Hot Pepper Sauce

and dentures
and this summoning of
who he was, existing
without who he is now,
which is why I need to remember

who I am now —
I can buy Wray and Nephews
because I am not under 21,
in the morning, I scrape a razor
along my jaw,

I can swear all I want
in the shower,
like my father
isn't boxed
on the shelf or in the ground.

Goodnight Africa Man

I won't say much.
You're the poet. I'm the carer
who says goodnight to
dementia patients. Makes
sure they've swallowed their
medication. Turns out lights.
I like England because my dreams
are different here, I mean
that they are comfortable.
I wake up younger
if I think about Lucinda,
the Jamaican lady in the wheelchair,
seventy-nine years in her body,
one leg cut off from diabetes
but missing no happiness.
Like a child when she sees me,
enough watts in her face
to light up huts in a forest.
Every night she says
hello Africa Man!
calls me happiest neighbour.
Her brain tells her
it is nineteen sixty-something
in Montego Bay
and she is living
with her father
who is a butcher: that's dementia,
an illness with a cleaver.
She asks when her father's coming back,
I say soon and she sits there
looking soulful.
One night she asked

if I've seen many oceans,
I said that there aren't any oceans
in Uganda, just lakes and I never had time
to visit them; she said
there is always enough time
in our lives to see
what we must see.

To Sweeten Bitter

My father had four children
and three sugars in his coffee
and every birthday he bought me
a dictionary which got thicker
and thicker and because his word
is not dead, I carry it like sugar

on a silver spoon
up the Mobay hills in Jamaica
past the flaked white walls
of plantation houses
past canefields and coconut trees
past the new crystal sugar factories

I ask dictionary why we came here
it said *nourish* so I sat with my aunt
on her balcony at the top
of Barnet Heights
and ate salt fish
and sweet potato

and watched women
leading their children
home from school
as I ate I asked dictionary
what is difficult about love?
It opened on the word *grasp*

and I looked at my hand
holding this ivory knife
and thought about how hard it was
to accept my father
for who he was
and where he came from

how easy it is now to spill
sugar on the table before
it is poured into my cup.

Recognising Leon

I am nineteen, still bitter as chalk dust
and working at the local gym
when I recognise you.

It's been seven years since
I saw your eyes,
red-striped lazy

in the windscreen mirror,
driving me to school,
calling my mum a whore.

My sister's phone call promised
not to come home if that man
was still sleeping in our mum's bed.

Now I'm six foot and I recognise you
despite your lost spine and loose face
but you don't recognise me.

I recognise the chance to pop
your mouth and beat you open.
Instead, I tell you about memberships

because I recognise
I am looking at a window
with the glass already smashed.

Jamaican British

after Arron Samuels

Some people would deny that I'm Jamaican British.
Angelo nose. Hair straight. No way I can be Jamaican British.

They think I say I'm black when I say Jamaican British
but the English boys at school made me choose Jamaican, British?

Half-caste, half mule, house slave - Jamaican British.
Light skin, straight male, privileged - Jamaican British.

Eat callaloo, plantain, jerk chicken - I'm Jamaican
British don't know how to serve our dishes, they enslaved us.

In school I fought a boy in the lunch hall - Jamaican.
At home, told Dad I hate *dem*, all d*em Jamaicans* — I'm British.

He laughed, said *you cannot love sugar and hate your sweetness*,
took me straight to Jamaica — passport, British.

Cousins in Kingston called me Jah-English,
proud to have someone in their family — British.

Plantation lineage, World War service, how do I serve Jamaican British?
When knowing how to war is Jamaican
British.

Miami Airport

why didn't you answer me back there?

you know how loud these things are on my waist?

you don't look deaf?

can you prove it?

do you know sign language?

I.D?

why didn't I see anyone that looked like you when I was in England?

why were you in Africa?

why don't you look like a teacher?

who are these photos of?

is this your girlfriend?

why doesn't she look English?

what was the address you stayed at?

what is the colour
of the bag you checked in?

what was your address again?

is that where we're going to find dope?

why are you checking your phone?

can I take your fingerprints?

why are your palms sweating?

you always look this lost?

why did you tell me your bag was red?

how did it change colour?

what colour are your eyes?

how much dope will I find in your bag?

why isn't there dope in your bag?

why did you confuse me?

why did you act strange when there was nothing on you?

would you believe
        what I've seen in the bags of people like you?

you think you're going
        to go free?

what did you not hear?

Give

I want to climb towards him, the one who is not in the ground. He is sat somewhere with his brother scooping jelly from the inside of a coconut. White afro comb, Vaseline and blue ironed shirts, looking sharp as the grief that drapes my body. If he saw his shirts on my back and his afro comb in my hair, he would stroke his white beard and call me *revivalist*.

Away

It's the grief talking, asking the dead why they aren't here. That's all it wants to know. I have his shirt, I even kept the ones he never wore, the green one that shrunk and smells of mothballs in closed cupboards.

His Clothes

Give away his clothes
all things of his will still fit
in this jumbled world.

Two Days And Two Nights In Kisumu, Kenya

The world in English has sharp edges — Binyavanga Wainaina

Day One

The classroom is an open-air hut,
84 children on chairs and low brick walls.
I walk in reeking of the road.
There's a gap in the roof where sunlight
beams onto my forehead.
Hello, I say. *Jambo Bwana*, the class says.
Dan explains, the kids speak Luo and Kiswahili
so he will need to translate.
Even the poets I met in Cape Town
would call this village *the real Africa*
not because the children don't have shoes (they do)
but because there are no hotels
or British schools or Chinese Casinos.
Shannon, a girl in a faded Man United shirt
asks how I become a poet.
I start talking in a language distant
until Dan carries my story in his tongue.

Night One

Barack Obama is "part-Kenyan" and has an "ancestral" hatred of Britain
— Boris Johnson

I lie in the candlelit hut
thinking how English
would never be the right tongue
to ask this class what matters.
I wonder what if no European
discovered anything in Kenya?

What if there was no brutal history
to speaking and writing English?
Would they still have
colonised the classroom?

Ben

        John   David

                    Christine   Hayley

Toby

Day 2

Wat a devilment a Englan!
Dem face war and brave de worse
But me wonderin how dem gwine stan
Colonizin in reverse — Louise Bennett

We are more interested in the future than the past —
David Cameron on reparations for the Transatlantic slave trade

After hearing Cameron on the radio
I dreamt of Uhuru Kenyatta refusing
to apologise for Africa's role in slavery
and under-developing Europe
because Africa is
more interested in the future.

I wake to say that even though I have come
to teach poetry, and not history,
our language has not come from the future,
it has crawled from a cave
and rowed to so many shores
that we speak in crashed waves and trade winds.

Night 2

The problem is not that we were once in charge [in Africa] but that we are not in charge any more — Boris Johnson

Dan, the Kenyan teacher, drives me to the airport
past Lake Victoria.
I ask him if he knows
the name of that lake
before 1858. He says I could tell you
but it has no meaning in English.

When He Died

I told no one
how old he was,
in case
his death
seemed too
inevitable.
When asked
his age, I made
him years younger,
needing
their
understanding –
he was taken
from me
too soon.

On A Boat, Zipping The Black River In Jamaica

A colony has no resource value for itself.
A colony never redeems itself with payment,
it merely receives — James Berry

Me, Thomas, Sam and Marcus, cameras around our necks, looking at
Shot — a young Jamaican boatman, slowing the boat, rolling a spliff to pass
around until everything floats. With our pores full of this salt, Shot points
at the bright bank of canefields,

green shocks from the ground, says *this was a floating plantation* and no one
knew if he was talking about this one field or the entire island, either way,
the observation put something in the air.

When a crocodile surfaces, its black bead eyes hold us like we are
everything and nothing and we are all light heads, mesmerized by its jaws,
teeth hidden below water, Shot says *that is the American Crocodile* and we all
pretend it's safe enough to laugh.

Dementia

Black with widening amnesia — Derek Walcott

When his sleeping face
was a scrunched tissue,
wet with babbling,

you came, unraveling a joy,
making him euphoric, dribbling
from his mouth

you simplified a complicated man,
swallowed his past
until your breath was
warm as Caribbean
concrete

O tender syndrome
steady in his greying eyes
fading song
in his grand dancehall

if you must,
do your gentle magic,
but make me unafraid
of what is

disappearing.

Kingston To Morant Bay

Di whole a Jamaica a capture land — Chronixx

I am the passenger writing down the names of Jamaican avenues in
Saint Thomas Parish - *Finchley, Golders Green, Surrey, Edgware*. Me and
Mike are two hours into driving through the island which smells like
cement and wet wood fire and we stop at a petrol station and a woman
holding a red umbrella, whose name I don't catch, asks *why you on road
and not on beach?* and I say *I'm from England, there's too much to see* and she
laughs and says but the roads are boring, we drive with a full tank, past
green guts of bamboo and coconuts, men grilling chicken, steam like
something slit the air's neck. We follow our red Google map arrow
into the Morant Bay mountains and the red dot disappears as if the
signal was a finger without strength to point. This is the birthplace of
Paul Bogle, a man with a smooth stone face who armed peasants with
machetes pointed at government men. The red dot suddenly reappears,
says *you have arrived at your destination*. We are 250 years away from the
hanging of Paul Bogle. Mike says *it doesn't look like we're anywhere* because
the road is pebbled and narrow, as if the road itself rebelled and gave
up making way for those who've forgotten what swung in this wind.

To Say

Where are the sofas from our childhood?
were the sofas ever unhappy?
didn't they ever want to run away?

what is the right thing to say
to my sister now she is happy?

what is the right
thing to cook when
my sister wants a meal?

what do I chop off when she
wants what she has given me back?

I am not saying any of this –
so why is she crying?

nothing is my fault, it doesn't
matter if I ever called her
bitch or she pretended
I was adopted.

nothing she says will make it untrue
that love sits on this sofa and becomes
her brother, deserving the plantain
our mother is cooking.

Scratched Light

for Phoebe Boswell

The heart is circled by sorrows and bitter devotion — Derek Walcott

Southbank's Security guards wake anyone sleeping
as if they don't want us to miss
who we might bump into
like how I bumped into Phoebe today,
sat at the tall window,
drawing a man called Anwaar.

I pull an extra chair and sit next to them
and talk about maybe moving out of London.

Everything about Phoebe stays on the paper.
        Curving Anwaar's left eye
she journeys the pencil in a circle —
finding something
but losing something else
in every new expression of Anwaar's face,
which is softer by the time he says *I miss Barbados,
my ex-wife, my children.*

He tears a Tate and Lyle sugar sachet
as Phoebe's hands press harder into his face.
We could all be crying or laughing
as the sun whips through the window
overlooking old stone banks and insurance offices.

We both hear the etching
while watching how Phoebe loosens
the grip on her pencil.
Anwaar asks who is holding me at night

I tell him half truths — *no one,*
I wake alone, I miss my ex,
my grandmother, my father.

There is nothing in my cup to spill when I tell him
that grief has moved me back in with mum.
Anwaar tells me about Swaziland and
Switzerland and places we could all be
if the right things stayed together.

      Phoebe finishes sketching the shape of the wall
      and the light and shade of his eye,

and now she looks up
seeing both of us for the first time
as men
      in the scratched light.

Look, There's A Black Man, Touch Him

They'd stroke my hand, poke my shoulders and run away
believing they'd dipped their snooping fingers into a kind
of exotic. An Irish man from Brooklyn got me a job in a garage,
called me his crumb brother. Helped me bowl spanners across
greased heads of snarling teddy boys. One night in a bar fight
a guy unzipped his stomach with a blade, my crumb brother
died and I lost everything on my plate. Came to London, tried
decorator work, had people turn me away for showing up
the wrong colour. Asking English people if they wanted me
to paint myself white, they called me racist. I was confused.
Got a job painting a school, I used the kind of blue you see in
St Elizabeth's Black River, corridors, Treasure Beach yellow,
doorframes, sugarcane green, you should have seen how the
English kids wanted to touch them.

Lifeguard

The doctor asks my dad
if he remembers
who he is.

His tongue, without strength to lift
him from where he's sunk
to the bottom of his brain.

I want to dive into the black
and grey pool of his medicated eyes
to save my dad's breath

by speaking for him.
I tell the doctor
he is my dad

but the doctor looks at me
like I rescued somebody
already drowned.

In The Classroom

with thanks to the voices in class 10P1 at Cardinal Pole Secondary, discussing the character 'Crooks' from *Of Mice & Men* by John Steinbeck.

1.

When we learnt about slavery our teacher couldn't point at Africa without eyes that gave us lashes, why begin our history with the shackle? One time, analysing some dead white man poem, he said *the mood in this poem is dark, what else can we associate with dark?* and I didn't want anyone anywhere to say *dirt* when they could say *the soil that flooded The River Nile*, didn't want to be marked the complexion of trouble, the companion of devils, not when I could be the ebony birthmark of written language - the eyeshadow of Egypt, the caviar of rebellion, the black and red gowns that lorded European royalists.

2.

Police pull me over for being a suspect of my own shade, ask me why and I'll show you how to look like something to be afraid of. We're killed in custody by the descendants of colonialists. It is in their blood to get away with murder.

3.

I like Jay-Z for capitalising on the N-word, giving us the concept of *successful Niggas in European cities*. No, I don't know who Richard Pryor is or why he never used the word *nigger* again after visiting Africa, but he was spelling the word, N-I-G-G-E-R, we say N-I-G-G-A, it is a deliberate trip-wire word in the mouth of white people who love Hip-Hop. As long as you say it like an American rapper, the word doesn't make me think of slavery. That whip is stretched too far back in time to slash our 21st Century backs, to not say the word is to act like we have not come far enough to be Presidents,   or Niggas.

The Day Is All Over Me Until I Find That Place

that beach, those feet, that blue, that air,
the moment that is and is not breathing
and I know how hard it is to get into the spot
that says sleep

it is ok, you are safe, your mother
is coming home, your father is already dead.
He no longer needs comfort, not while
I'm here with another cupboard
and a set of clothes to put on
to walk around in

like everyone with two arms,
legs and a heartbeat. I can't make importance out of
sense. Can't make sense of the turning
and the losing of myself, and finding
the kind of universe where people sit
crossed-legged under bridges and spit
into rivers. In my head
I am sitting down too. This is how far I have
to come away from myself   to be with myself.
To know that breath always finds its depth
in the calm ground of every

earthly

silence.

What Is Possible

is that I will fly and I grow too big for my bed
like dreams have stretched me into a giant.
I cannot get enough sleep
because it is late, the TV is on downstairs
and I can hear it even though my hearing aids
are not in. I will complain about it
in the morning and mum will ask
why my hearing gets better at night.
It will take me another ten years
to appreciate how hard she has worked
to keep me warm in a house
it is true that I am held together by her love
but that string is buried too deep
inside me to pluck and say ah yes
I am only fully alive if you are.
I am in bed and there are stickers glowing
on the ceiling
so it is never completely dark
because I used to be afraid of it
but I have become friends with the dark
because it keeps me hidden
while I think about a girl I like who is not here
though I wish she was, we could do stuff
I don't yet know how to do.
It is possible I am going to wake up
a white American man like Tom Hanks
because I just saw the film *Big*,
I would do anything to dance
on giant piano keys playing 'Heart and Soul'.
It is possible that the only thing
that separates me from another universe
is the window I sleep next to.

It is possible that I know what is out there
and I can feel something inside my gut has legs
and is kicking saying, 'We can go anywhere
when we wake tomorrow morning.'
It is possible that I am just trying
to sleep inside myself and this
is the most peaceful sleep I will ever have.
The TV on downstairs while mum works
through the night threading jewellery
to sell at the weekend market. Sounds
muffle through floorboards,
my big sister in the bedroom upstairs.
I can't hear her but I know she is there —
she will wake up tomorrow morning
it is impossible that she won't.

It is possible I will fall
out of my skin and the dream will become
something I walk around in.

Bottomless

i. A Dark And Bitter Thing

When my dad gives me
my first sip of his Guinness
I suck up a face
that does not know
what to do with the taste.

ii. In Mum's Kitchen

My birthday boy face
glimmers
when the lights
turn off.
There is no shape
of my dad in the dark.
My yellow badge says
I am 6 today
and the burst
rubber balloons say
I am a love child,
everything about me
is accidental.

iii. Music

My mum cleans the kitchen,
opens all the windows, blaring
mixtapes dad made in the 80s.
The ones he would bring round
after he beat her.
His smooth DJ voice croons
Ain't Nobody's Fault But Mine
from the tape deck, treating
the wound with music.
In a year she'll leave him
but for now she sings along,
sweeping cake crumbs
under the table.

iv. Running Away

When mum took us
to run away from dad,
my sister's eyes formed search parties.
Who calls their children
on their summer holidays to say,
know what I'm going to do?
I'm going to burn the house down.

v. My Dad Drunk

Said he was ashamed
to have white children.
Which was confusing
because when sober
he called me black.

Maybe I became
an uptown shade —
ghosts
he saw
in the white foam
of his drained pint glass.

vi. Promise

Watching him sleep
in his hospital bed,
a thought rises in me -
a black mouthful
of things I have been
trying to keep down since
childhood. I realise that
I have always forgiven him
for everything, because
he promised me one
day he was going to die.

I want to bury the sounds of living
in his ears with the birds,

and every little thing with a song,
where nothing is heavy like this place,

where someone I love is the shape
of   a   missing   thing.

Notes on the poems

In The Supermarket has a ghost poem in italics.

To Sweeten Bitter came out of an Oblique Strategy exercise using the first words I flicked to at random in my Dad's dictionary.

Give Away His Clothes is a variation of a Haibun.

Recognising Leon was inspired by the poet Mark Turcotte.

Jamaican British is a Broken Ghazal inspired by Arron Samuels.

Scratched Light was commissioned by Jay Bird Live Literature for National Poetry Day, responding to early - late afternoon light and was partly inspired by the poem *Light Of The World* by Derek Walcott. Phoebe Boswell is a Kenyan-British artist and film maker based in London.

Look There's A Black Man Touch Him is an adaptation of my Dad's story arriving in the UK.

In The Classroom is in the voice of a number of year 10 students at Cardinal Pole Catholic School in Hackney who were debating the use of the word "nigger" in Of Mice And Men by John Steinbeck after one student threw the book across the room and refused to carry on reading it.

The original title for this collection was *The Island That's Hard To Find In English*. I went exploring in Liverpool, Hull, London, Bristol and other parts of the UK significant to Britain's role in the Transatlantic slave trade.

You can watch an animated version of *Sestina To My Father* (The Island That's Hard To Find In English) at www.raymondantrobus.com

Acknowledgements

Some of these poems or earlier versions of them have appeared in
*The Rialto, Magma, Morning Star, Oxford Diaspora's Programme, British Council
Literature, Shooter Literary Journal, And Other Poems, Media Diversified* and
forthcoming in *Wasafiri, Bare Lit Anthology* and *Bloodaxe Ten Anthology.*

Big up Jack Underwood, Hannah Lowe, Anthony Anaxagorou, Shira
Erlichman, Simon Mole, Keith Jarrett, Indigo Williams, Peter Kahn,
Mike Rahfaldt and Rachel Long for their advice and encouragement.

Special big up to Out-Spoken Press for giving these poems a home.

Bio

Raymond Antrobus is a British-Jamaican poet, performer and educator, born and bred in East London, Hackney. He is one of the world's first recipients of an in Spoken Word education from Goldsmiths University.

His poems have been published in magazines and literary journals such as POETRY magazine (US), Poetry Review, The Rialto, Magma Poetry, Oxford Diaspora's Programme, British Council Literature, Shooter Literary Journal, The Missing Slate, Morning Star, Media Diversified, The Deaf Poet's Society and forthcoming in Wasafiri, University Of Arkansas Press and Bloodaxe, Ten Anthology.

His first pamphlet – *Shapes & Disfigurements of Raymond Antrobus* (2012) - is published by Burning Eye Books. His second pamphlet, *To Sweeten Bitter* (2017) is published by Out-Spoken Press. His debut poetry collection will be published by Penned In The Margins (2018).

Raymond has read and performed his poetry at festivals (Glastonbury, Latitude, Bestival etc) to universities (Oxford, Goldsmiths, Warrick etc). He has won numerous slams (Farrago International Slam Champion 2010, The Canterbury Slam 2013 and was runner up at the open mic Calabash Slam in 2016). He has also read internationally (South Africa, Kenya, North America, Jamaica, Sweden, Italy, Germany, Switzerland etc).

Raymond is co-curator of popular London poetry events *Chill Pill* (Soho Theatre and The Albany) and *Keats House Poets Forum*. Raymond's poetry has appeared on BBC 2, BBC Radio 4, The Big Issue, The Jamaica Gleaner, The Guardian and at TedxEastEnd.

Sky Arts and Ideas Tap listed Raymond in the top 20 promising young artists in the UK. The Fadar listed Raymond as a Writer Of Colour to watch in 2017.

He is currently a Complete Works III fellow and freelance teacher.

Raymond completed his Creative Writing & Education MA with a distinction.

Other titles by Out-Spoken Press:

Dogtooth
Fran Lock

From the lines of Dissent
Media Diversified

How You Might Know Me
Sabrina Mahfouz

Heterogeneous
New & Selected Poems
Anthony Anaxagorou

Titanic
Bridget Minamore

A Heartful of Fist
A SLAMbassadors Anthology 2016
Poetry Society & Out-Spoken Press

Out-Spoken 2015
An Anthology of Poetry
Out-Spoken Press

A Difficult Place To Be Human
Anthony Anaxagorou

A Silence You Can Carry
Hibaq Osman

outspokenldn@gmail.com